From:

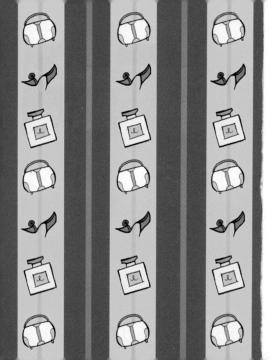

What Every Woman Should Do Once

Claudine Gandolfi
Illustrated by Kerrie Hess

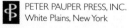

PETER PAUPER PRESS, INC.
White Plains, New York

Illustrations copyright 2004 © Kerrie Hess/
www.artscounselinc.com

Designed by Heather Zschock

Copyright © 2004
Peter Pauper Press, Inc.
202 Mamaroneck Avenue
White Plains, NY 10601
ISBN 1-59359-950-1
Printed in China
7 6 5 4 3 2 1

Visit us at www.peterpauper.com

What Every Woman Should Do Once

Make up
an alias

Skinny dip

Insist on
being called
"Your Majesty"

Be a diva for
a night at a
karaoke bar

Act out a
page of the
Kama Sutra

Call in sick and
spend a whole
day shopping with
your best friend

Own something
leather, besides a
coat or gloves

Date a guy
you met on the
Internet

Dye your hair
blonde and see if
they really do
have more fun

Rent a convertible
and go where the
wind blows

Adopt
a pet

Go commando

Try on engagement rings, even if you're not in a relationship

Ask a man out

Buy a
really racy
piece of
lingerie

Invest in
a high risk
stock

Send
yourself a
dozen roses

Audition for a
Broadway musical
or a TV
Reality Show

Bet it all on
black in Vegas—
and let it ride

Go on a carriage
ride through
Central Park

Try on very expensive clothes in a boutique that you know you can't afford

Invent an interesting past

Buy a round for
everyone in the bar

Smoke a
cigar

Pamper

yourself at an

all day spa

Have a three martini
lunch and go back to
work refreshed

Create your
own holiday
and celebrate it
every year

Wear fake eyelashes
and send him come
hither looks

Make a
voodoo doll
of your ex

Learn to tango

Pretend you're a
food critic at a
trendy restaurant

Make snow angels

Hire a
personal
shopper

Wear a feather boa
and movie star glasses
to the grocery store

Borrow a motorcycle and take the driver's seat

Invest in a
piece of art

Flirt your
way through a
traffic jam

Taste every
variety of
margarita

Kiss a guy from
every state

Throw a silk pajama party and greet guests with a glass of champagne

Go on two
dates in
one night

Volunteer
at a homeless
shelter

Take the credit,
and the compliments,
and say thanks!

Send a thank you letter to a mentor

Resist saying,
"I told you so," even
when you're right

Head to
the airport
and fly—
anywhere

Walk a mile
in someone
else's shoes

Ask your boyfriend to paint your toenails in exchange for the remote

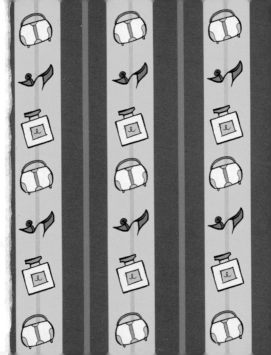

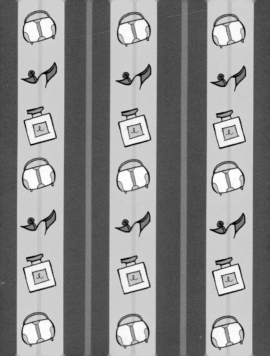